How To Buy A House

First Time Home Buyer's Quick And
Easy Guide To Buying A Home

Jeff Leighton

Table of Contents

Introduction

Buying a house is the largest investment of most people's lives. The more educated you are in the process, the more you'll be able to make good choices when it comes to home ownership. This guide will take you through everything you need to know about the home-buying process, step by step. As a real estate agent and investor I have seen hundreds of real estate deals ranging from fixer upper homes to ultra-luxury estates and everything in between. In this book, we'll go over the most important parts of the homebuying process and the situations you should try to avoid. As long as you are informed and find a good agent, both of which we will cover in this book, your home-buying process should be smooth and rewarding.

CHAPTER 1

Steps To Buying A House

Step 1: Research

The first thing you do in your house search, before even contacting a real estate agent, should be to start driving around neighborhoods and doing research on different areas to find out in what areas you would potentially want to live. Local articles, listservs, and even forums can give you a good idea of the type of neighborhood and its houses.

I would even recommend checking out areas that are not at the top of your list, just to be sure. I can't tell you how many times I have worked with a client who is initially only looking at one area but eventually decides that another neighborhood not originally on their radar is the one they want. The same is true with the style of house. Some people initially only want a colonial, but might prefer a modern rambler once they start viewing homes in person. You should browse around on free real estate websites like Redfin or Zillow as much as possible to get an idea of the style of houses, prices, how fast they typically sell, and other general information before viewing any.

Once you have done a lot of online research and driven through neighborhoods, the next step would be to start going to open houses. You do not need a real estate agent to attend open houses, and you should see at least 10-25 open houses of different styles and price ranges so that you really know what you are looking for. You are now in the hunt for a house and probably more informed than most homebuyers out there, maybe even more than some real estate agents. Feel free to watch as much HGTV as possible too. The shows are fairly realistic, and you can learn some good house-buying tips. Also, it might be a good idea to talk to any friends or family that have recently bought houses. Maybe take them out for coffee, dinner, or even a happy hour and pick their brains about the house-buying process. You never know what interesting tips or stories you might hear.

Step 2: Get Your Finances in Order

The next step in your house-buying journey is to get your finances in order as much as possible. This will determine how much you can afford. In the period when you want to buy a house, try not to make any other large purchases that may affect your credit or income qualifications. You should try to pay down any existing debt you have and check your credit score for any mistakes. Having a high credit score will affect your interest rate and, ultimately, your monthly payment. Start saving up for a down payment as well. You may not be aware of it, but there are many different types of loans you can get for a house. Fortunately, if you are a first-time homebuyer, you only have to put down 3.5 to 5%, if you choose to. That does not include closing costs, which is an additional 2.5 to 3.5% out of your pocket, but don't think that you need 20% down or anything to buy your first home.

Even if you decide to put down 3.5 to 5% on your first home, keep in mind that with owning a home you always want to have a reserve fund for things that can go wrong. This isn't like an apartment where you just call the maintenance guy who fixes the problem. You have to pay any expense out of your own pocket, and I can guarantee you there will be surprises along the way. Your local real estate agent should have a list of recommended contractors that they can give you. If they don't, then just browse around on the top real estate agent's websites in your area. Their website usually contains a section called "preferred vendors or recommended contractors", and you can just go with those. Neighborhood listservs can often also be a great place to find resources like contractors and others.

The bottom line is that you need to save up as much as possible, pay down any debt, and get your credit score as high as it can possibly be.

Step 3: Get Pre-Approved

The next step in your home-buying journey is to get pre-approved by a lender. Keep in mind too that there is a big difference between a pre-approval and a prequalification letter from your lender. A prequalification is the initial estimate that you may get from a lender without them verifying any paperwork. The rule of thumb for how much mortgage you can afford is usually 2.5 times your annual gross salary. However, it is not uncommon for people to buy houses at 3, 4, and, in some cases, even 5 times their annual gross salary. It depends on how much money you are bringing to the table, interest rates, and the type of loan you get. When you're getting your pre-approval, your lender will typically ask for things like your income, assets, debt, and credit score. As long as you are straightforward about things, there should not be any issues. However, most agents will not take a prequalification seriously. Anytime you make an offer, and before you really start looking at houses, you need to have a pre-approval, which is one step beyond a prequalification. At that point you actually fill out a loan application and get a conditional approval letter stating how much you can afford. The lender will verify your credit score, and you will need to provide at least two years of tax returns and two months of asset account statements. When you're making an offer on a property, a pre-approval looks much stronger in the eyes of the seller than a prequalification.

There are plenty of lenders out there, both online and locally, that you can choose from. Based on my own experience with hundreds of deals, I would say you should get a local lender. A local lender with a good reputation that a listing agent can call and talk to, almost always looks stronger than an online lender in terms of an offer. People regularly get a slightly better rate with an online lender halfway across the country. However, in my experience, the service and quality will be much worse. Whenever you call them, you get directed to a 1-800 number and go through a call center just to get in touch with someone. If something happens along the way to your house purchase or you need to get a quick response from an online lender, all I can say is: good luck. Having a local lender with a local cell phone and a good reputation is the way to go. You may pay a slightly higher rate; however, the likelihood of the loan going through on time is significantly higher. I have seen delays with online lenders that can put your earnest money deposit – and the entire deal – at risk.

OK, my rant is over, but once you are pre-approved by a local lender, the next step is to choose a real estate agent. Keep in mind too that just because you are approved for 200K or 500K, that does not mean you have to purchase a place at that price. It is simply the maximum the lender will allow. There is something to be said for buying a place a little bit under your budget and having more money on hand every month for projects, or just for fun and travels. You don't want to be stretched too thin just to show off that you can afford a nicer house.

Step 4: Find the Right Real Estate Agent

Finding the right real estate agent is a major key in your home-buying process. Although you should already be fairly educated in the home-buying process from doing research, attending open houses, and speaking with friends, a good real estate agent can help you get the deal done for a good price.

The best way to find a good agent is a combination of referrals and online research. You should ask your lender about any good agents, as well as friends and family about who they used and who they would recommend. Since there are so many agents out there, you want someone that comes highly recommended and has experience in the type of property and price range that you are looking for. Some people like to shop around and interview many agents before selecting one, while others just choose the first one that pops up in an online search. If you are more meticulous, then maybe you could interview several. However, my recommendation would be to get a couple of recommendations/referrals from either a friend or a lender, and then look up the people online to check their reviews. If they come highly recommended and they have great reviews online, then that is usually good enough for me, and I would select one just based on that.

I typically do not have people sign buyer agency agreements, although some agents may require that you sign an agreement with them for six months or so. That means that any offer you make, has to go through them. Again, if they come highly recommended and they have a lot of good reviews online, then I wouldn't have an issue signing one of those. However, most agents I know do not get their clients to sign these.

Once you start working with that agent, they will typically set you up with an MLS search around the types of properties, price range, and location of what you are looking for. As an agent, I can tell you that I prefer to show homes with a little bit of notice and all at the same time. Usually, you'll want to schedule anywhere from three to five homes for a given showing time, instead of just seeing one house here and there. Real estate is often last-minute, and when a house pops up, it may need to be seen ASAP, since it could sell quickly. That is why I would recommend working with an agent that has a team. It increases the odds that several different agents could get out there quickly and show you the home. You need your agent to be flexible and responsive with showings, as well as with writing offers.

Step 5: Making Offers That Win

Once you have done your own research, got pre-approved, and found a real estate agent, the next step is to narrow down on the properties you could be interested in and start making offers. At this point, you should know exactly what you are looking for and be set up for updates from your agent on any new listings as soon as they hit the market. Keep in mind that if you are in a competitive market, it is not uncommon to bid on multiple houses to get one accepted. I have listed some tips here for making a strong offer, especially in a multiple-offer scenario.

When you submit your offer, you should be approved by a local lender with a good reputation. Many listing agents are weary of accepting offers from online lenders with a 1-800 number and no customer service. It may be tempting to use an online lender, since sometimes you can get slightly lower rates. However, it will make your offer look weaker because the likelihood of the loan coming through on your closing date is much lower than if you'd gone with a local lender that you can call or email personally.

Another tip is to remove your financing contingency. You should only do this if you have talked with your lender and are confident your loan will not get rejected. Keep in mind that if you have already been pre-approved, then your loan should not get rejected and dropping this contingency can make your offer look much stronger. You can also increase your EMD or earnest money deposit. Putting a larger percent down for your initial deposit can show that you are more serious about the house. The usual amount is 1-3% of the purchase price; however, you could put down upwards of 5% or more.

Another contingency you could consider waiving, is the home inspection contingency. Anytime you buy a house, you typically do a home inspection where an inspector might spend three hours going through the house looking for items that need repair. At the end of the inspection, the inspector typically has a 30-page report detailing all the items that need repair. In a super competitive market, you could consider waiving this contingency or just doing a modified home inspection, where you don't ask for any items to be fixed, but you still have the option to cancel it if it looks like there might be too much work. Both of these are common and give the seller much more peace of mind than a standard home inspection, where they might have to hire contractors or give credits to fix different items. I have also seen success with doing a pre-inspection where you pay an inspector to do an inspection before you have the property under contract. When you then make your offer, you can remove your home inspection contingency, since you know the house might not need that much work. This strategy is best for multiple-offer situations. If the house has been on the market for a while and there are no other offers, then you should stick with a standard home inspection.

The last inspection you could consider waiving is the appraisal contingency. This is the riskiest of all the contingencies, because if the property does not appraise, then you have to pay the difference. However, if there are a lot of comps that would support the price the seller is looking for, this can be a great option that makes your offer stand out. You could also do a so-called 'partial appraisal contingency', where you put in that the property just needs to appraise for at least a certain amount but not necessarily the offer price.

In addition to dropping or modifying contingencies, you can also appeal to the seller on a personal level. Writing a letter to the seller describing who you are and what you are looking for in a house can be a great tool that has worked wonders in the past. If you have a family, you can even include a picture and talk about how excited you are to start a new chapter in your life. If you look online, there are many template letter examples for buying a house and appealing to the seller. We have won bids in the past where we did not have the highest offer, but because buying and selling a home can be such an emotional thing, the sellers appreciated the extra effort of the letter and went with us.

One of the most common techniques for making a strong offer and winning in a competitive situation is an escalation clause. This is a common technique where you say, "I will pay $1,000, $2,000, or $5,000 more than the closest offer, all the way up to the maximum price that would pay for the home." The good thing about these escalation clauses is that if the selling agent escalates to your highest price, then they have to show you the other offer that triggered your escalation. I have seen houses where it made sense to escalate 20K or even 50K over the asking price. Sometimes the agent will list the house artificially lower in hopes of generating a bidding war. That is why it helps to do research on the neighborhood so you know what houses are going for and you don't overpay. Keep in mind that you only need to do an escalation clause if there are multiple offers and you really don't want to lose the house. If there are no other offers, then just do a normal offer without the clause. You don't want the listing agent to know how much you are willing to pay for the home.

When making offers and winning bids, sometimes it will just come down to the price. However, the seller often also wants an offer from someone who is most likely to close and won't cause a lot of delays with inspections, headaches, and drama.

Step 6: EMD and Inspections

Once you have a property under contract, the next step is to deposit your EMD or earnest money deposit with the title company of choice based on your offer. The earnest money deposit will go towards your closing costs and is a required part of the home-buying process. It is usually anywhere from 2-5% of the purchase price. In many contracts you have to take care of this within 5 days of putting the property under contract, or technically your contract will not be valid.

You should also try to schedule your home inspections ASAP. Most home inspection contingencies only last a week or so, and sometimes inspectors are booked up for a while, so your real estate agent should have a list of recommended inspectors you can call and get out to the property. Do not wait until the last minute for home inspections, as you will need time to get the results back and then choose what you will ask for.

In many cases, it is not uncommon for an inspector to have a long list of items from the inspection report, especially if it is an older house. Keep in mind that nearly every house has a list of items. It can be a little intimidating to get your first report back and find 30 pages of repairs that might be needed. You want to make sure that you focus on the major items. It can be tempting to ask for the smaller items, but sometimes the seller will balk if you ask for too much. Usually, as long as both parties are reasonable, there is some negotiating about the inspection items, and you end up meeting in the middle. Sometimes the seller will prefer to offer a credit to fix any items, and sometimes they will offer to hire the contractors themselves – both ways can work. If the seller thinks you got a good deal or you are buying the house "as is", then there is often no negotiating with the home inspection – it's either take it or leave it. We have had many clients buy houses as is or with just a pass/fail inspection. Sometimes you can get really good deals that way, since most buyers prefer to look at homes in which they can do a traditional inspection.

With your home inspection, as long as the property is not a condo, you should also ask for a radon test. Radon is a gas that comes from the ground and is the second leading cause of lung cancer after smoking. It can be found in many houses that have basements. It is a fairly simple test to do and there is a fairly easy remediation if it is found. To remediate radon, you typically have a radon company install a PVC-like pipe into the sump pump or basement, which has a small fan inside of it that kicks out any radon. The radon systems also have a 24/7 measurement so that you can always be sure the radon system is working. In most scenarios the seller pays to install a radon system for you or give you a credit for it, which is usually in the ballpark of a thousand dollars.

Step 7: Financing

The next step after depositing your earnest money check and scheduling home and radon inspections is to work with your lender to get your financing locked in. The home inspection is usually the biggest hurdle; however, you need to be in constant communication with your lender to make sure they have everything they need and that you are on track to close on time. That means: do not make any large purchases, quit your job, or even change jobs during this time. It typically takes about 30 days to close on a property, depending on what you put in the contract, so be wary of any big financial moves during that time.

Some people we know even shop around lenders once they have a home under contract to see who can give them the best rate. If you decide to stick with your original lender or shop around a little bit, keep in mind that you need to order the appraisal in a timely manner because most contracts have about a three-week appraisal contingency. It can take a week or two to order and get an appraisal back, and if you don't submit it within the time frame, you risk having the deal fall apart. The main thing once you get a property under contract is to know the deadlines for your inspection contingency, financing contingency, and appraisal contingency.

Step 8: Get the Appraisal

Usually, within the first week or two of getting your offer accepted, you will need to order the appraisal. Most real estate contracts have an appraisal contingency of three to four weeks, and it can take a week to get the appraisal back, so be sure to order it in a timely fashion.

The appraisal is the estimate of a property's value, which is required by any lender before they provide you with a loan. They use a third party to do this appraisal because they want to make sure you are not overpaying for the home and that the property is worth at least what you have it under contract for. In the worst-case scenario, if you were to default on your home, then the lender would have to sell off the property to repay the loan, so that is why they require this. The appraised value of the home is based on things like square footage, the number of bedrooms and bathrooms, the neighborhood location, and any interior improvements. The appraiser will usually spend half an hour at the house under contract, and then go back to the office and look at several other homes in the neighborhood as a comparison for the value of your property. Keep that in mind when it comes to an appraisal.

Your lender will order the appraisal, and you will need to make sure that they do. Usually, an appraisal costs anywhere from $300 to $500, and you typically pay that out of pocket, although you can get it paid at the closing as well. Your lender is required to give you a copy of the appraisal as soon as they receive it so that you can understand how they came up with their appraisal value. The overwhelming majority of the time, the appraisal will come at the price you have the house under contract for. The lender's main focus is that the property is worth at least what you are paying for it. However, in some cases, the appraisal value can come back much higher or much lower than what you have it under contract for. If it comes back higher than what you have it under contract for, then that is a good sign that you got a great deal. Every now and then, I see that happen. However, if your appraisal comes back lower than your purchase price, then you have a couple of options. The bank has assisted you by making sure you are not paying too much for the house.

Almost every contract has an appraisal contingency, where you are allowed to make the seller drop their price to the appraised value or you can cancel the contract. The seller may or may not agree to this if you are in a hot market, so then it is up to you and your real estate agent to decide if you want to move forward or not. If you have waived the appraisal contingency to make your offer more attractive to the seller, then you may have to come out of pocket with cash to cover the difference between the appraised value and the price you have it under contract for. Sometimes I see cases where people will order a second appraisal or challenge the appraisal with different comparable sales. Most of the time a second appraisal or challenging the appraisal does not work, unless there is outright negligence by the appraiser. Usually, the seller drops their price to meet the appraised value, or they split the cost with the potential buyer.

Step 9: Final Walk-Through

The final walk-through of a house is usually conducted on the day of closing, or a day or two before. You walk through the house with the idea that the seller has moved everything out completely and has made any repairs from the home inspection that they were supposed to make. With most final walk-throughs, your agent will have a checklist of items to test, including everything from the HVAC, flushing toilets, and making sure the seller has not left anything or damaged the house during the move out.

If there were repairs done, this is the time to check on them, and the seller should have provided receipts via email or left the receipts at the house from a licensed contractor who is qualified to do that type of work. Occasionally, the seller will not have done all the repairs, or you may find that they have left items in the house that you need removed. That is why it's so important to do final walk-throughs. I would estimate that during about 1 in 10 walk-throughs, there may still be something unresolved. Most of the time it is nothing major, and you simply give an addendum to the contract saying that the seller will remove anything that they left, or that they will get a licensed contract or evaluate and repair any remaining issues. This addendum allows you to still close on time and then the seller would be required to fix any items.

In most states, the seller is supposed to leave the house in broom-swept condition, meaning they technically do not need to get it professionally cleaned before you move in, although sometimes sellers will hire a cleaning crew prior to closing. It is fairly common for there to be a little bit of dirt from all the moving, and sometimes small nail marks on the walls from frames and other furnishings. Most new buyers get new paint for a house anyways. Sometimes I see buyers do a walk-through a day or two before closing if there were a lot of items to be repaired. Keep in mind that final walk-throughs are not always a perfect process; however, in the rare instances where there is an issue, it typically gets worked out with a simple one-page addendum.

Step 10: Close the Deal

After all of your contingencies have been met and you have done the final walk-through, the next step is to go to your title company and sign the paperwork. Usually, once your property is under contract, you will be in touch with the title company every couple of days or so, because they typically will ask you to fill out different forms and make sure that everyone is on the same page. Closing is usually a straightforward process, and your lender is required by law to give you your final closing statements at least three days before closing so that you have time to review.

At the closing you will have to bring your photo ID, as well as a cashier, and a certified check to cover your down payment and closing costs. A typical closing will last 45-90 minutes, depending on what type of loan you have and how quickly you go through the documents. Nowadays, most closings are split so you will not be signing in the same room or at the same time as the seller. They do that because it's easier to have one party sign at a time, since you don't want to have to wait for someone else. At the closing, the title company will have you sign all the documents that they have examined to make sure your property has clean title, and you will be signing a large stack of loan documents.

Since you will be getting your closing documents several days before closing, you can feel free to call and ask the title company about any fees you are not sure about. You can also get free estimates from title companies in the beginning of the home-buying process since they will vary in price. This is one part of the home-buying process where I would go with the most reputable title company that your real estate agent knows. I would highly recommend spending a little extra and going with a professional title company that gets great reviews and has a lawyer on their staff. I have seen people try to use the cheapest title company, which usually causes delays and confusion. Overall, I have not had great experiences with the virtual title companies. You've signed the paperwork? Congratulations, you are done! You will get the keys right after signing everything. Now, you can finally relax.

CHAPTER 2

Tips for Buying a House

Tip 1

Look at a ton of houses before even choosing a real estate agent so that you know what a good deal is in your area. The one mistake I made when I bought my first condo was that I only looked at a couple of places before making a decision. You almost want to think of yourself as becoming a neighborhood expert, make it a game, see if you can even know more about your area and real estate than your local agent. Just by reading freely available articles online about neighborhoods, looking at listings online, and visiting lots of open houses, you can be more educated than the majority of homebuyers out there, even more than some real estate agents. When I look at investment deals with the investors I work with, they often say they look at 100 deals before choosing one. The investors really like to cherry-pick the best deals. Even though they are not physically driving to all those deals, they like to analyze and only choose the cream-of-the-crop properties.

Tip 2

If there is one thing I have learned about real estate over the last ten years, location is really everything. I know everyone has heard the phrase, "The three most important things in real estate are location, location, location," but I could not agree more. If you care about things like resale value and price appreciation, then make sure you buy in a convenient location. You don't know how many times I have seen someone purchase an amazing house with a huge yard in a brand new subdivision 30 or 40 minutes outside of the city, only to not see it appreciate whatsoever, and in some cases even drop in value. On the other hand, I have seen others who may purchase a small townhouse in an up-and-coming part of town in the city who see their values double or even triple. If you want your property to appreciate in value, then pay a little bit extra to live closer, in the city near where you work, or in a transitional neighborhood that is still within the city limits.

Tip 3

When you buy a house, unexpected expenses can always come up. It would be wise to have some money saved away for any repairs or work needed. That is not to say that your roof will need to be replaced tomorrow or anything like that, but you will sleep much easier at night knowing you have some money for projects around the house. You should probably save at least anywhere around 1-2% of the purchase price of the house in a reserve fund for unexpected expenses. If you are buying an older house, i.e. a house of more than 50 years old, then I would budget even more. Many times the older houses were built much better than houses today; however, 50 years is a long time for different systems and aspects of the house to start showing their wear and tear, so always plan for more.

Tip 4

If you are in a multiple-offer situation, which is common in many areas these days, you can do several things that we have done successfully to be the winning bidder, without having to pay too much for the property.

The first thing you can do is write a personal letter to the seller. This strategy works very well since sellers can often be very emotional about selling their home. There are plenty of freely available templates online for personal letters to sellers, and we have had a lot of success with that.

The next thing you can do is to either waive the home inspection completely or just do a pass/fail inspection, where you don't ask to negotiate for any items like you would on a traditional home purchase. You can often pay a home inspector a smaller fee than what they typically charge and do a so-called a 'pre-inspection' on a house. In this scenario the inspector might only spend an hour or so in the house and would only look for major items. If they tell you it's good, then you can waive the inspection completely and make your offer look much stronger than people with a traditional home inspection contingency.

The last thing I would suggest doing in a multiple-offer scenario is to be approved with a local lender as opposed to an online lender or some big bank. That can often be the difference if you have a couple of offers.

Tip 5

Drive through as many neighborhoods as possible to get a feel for the community, as well as an idea of the commuting times. Since you'll most likely live there for a while, you should know all the roads, estimated commutes, busy times for traffic in your area, and different options for commuting. I know some people who even make the drive or ride the train from the area where they would potentially be living in.

Tip 6

Utilize as many real estate apps as you can in your home search. Many of the apps give you just as much, if not more, information than your real estate agent might have. The more informed you are before you make your purchase, the better. Some of the top apps I would recommend downloading are the Redfin app, Zillow, and the Doorsteps Swipe app, to name a few.

Tip 7

Consider creating an Airbnb suite at your property. This does not typically work for condos, but if you buy a single-family home or a townhouse in or near a big city, you can create an Airbnb suite in your basement. Short-term rentals can often pay you significantly more than a traditional renter and can even cut your mortgage in half or allow you to live for free essentially.

There are plenty of resources online on how to best set up your Airbnb listing; however, Airbnb makes it easy to get your property listed and start making money off of it. The regulations on Airbnb are always changing, so be sure to stay up to date in your area. I would recommend reading success stories online about the best practices for maximizing income with Airbnb.

Tip 8

If you buy a fixer upper house, keep in mind that you can get a great deal. However, the repairs usually cost more than you are anticipating, and the process usually takes longer than expected. Unless you come from a construction background, I would recommend only buying a fixer upper that needs cosmetic repairs. When you do decide to fix it up, make sure to get a highly recommended contractor with a license and insurance, but also plan on the renovation costs to be anywhere from 10 to 25% more than you anticipated. Even the experienced investors I have worked with always add at least a 10% buffer to their repair costs.

Tip 9

Always think of your home's resale value. Sometimes houses on busy roads, in front of schools, or in livable but close-to-tear-down condition might seem like a steal of deal. However, although the prices might seem very low compared to the rest of the neighborhood, the market for someone who would purchase a house on a busy road, in front of a school, or in barely livable conditions is much smaller than the market of people looking for a normal house in a good neighborhood. Any of those factors can turn a buyer off completely, since most people are looking for homes in move-in condition on a quieter street. We once had a buyer who bought a house against our recommendation on one of the busiest roads, directly in front of a school, and in near tear-down condition. All I can say to them is: good luck selling the property. It will most likely sit on the market for months on end given its location.

Tip 10

When choosing a title company to go with, get a recommendation from your real estate agent. As long as your agent has done a good number of deals, they will direct you to the best title company they know of. You can often shop around and find less expensive title companies; however, sometimes the drop in service quality can be astonishing. I will tell you a quick horror story. Most title companies have a professional office with a lawyer and maybe a couple of rooms to do closings. I remember we had one client who wanted to save several hundred dollars in closing fees, so he went with a virtual title company that would meet us wherever we wanted. All I can say is that the guy who showed up to do our closing not only showed up almost an hour late, but was also wearing a soccer jersey and carrying a suitcase. The entire time he was doing the closing, he was on the phone with some title attorney in a completely different state who was walking him through what to do. This may even have been his first closing, for all I know. The entire closing took almost two hours, which is unheard of and jeopardized the deal going through. That being said, pay a little bit extra and go with someone your agent refers you to.

CHAPTER 3

Common Mistakes When Buying Your First House

Mistake 1: Trying to Buy Without an Agent

I don't care how much HGTV you watch or how many summer jobs you worked fixing up your neighbor's house – you need a real estate agent. Even the most mediocre real estate agent is better for you than trying to do it alone. Many unrepresented buyers are not taken seriously by the listing agent, and if they are, the listing agent knows they can probably get them to come up significantly on price or to significantly lower the standard contingencies. You need someone in your corner who has your best interests in mind, i.e. a buyer's agent. When buying a house, you want every advantage going for you. Having a real estate agent will help.

Mistake 2: Not Thinking About Resale Value

At some point in your life, you will most likely sell the property you are considering to buy. With that in mind, you always need to think about resale value. I would recommend not buying property on extremely busy roads, in front of schools, or in tear-down conditions that are barely livable. The first house I bought was a studio condo. Even though I bought it at a downturn in the economy, the property did not appreciate that much when I went to sell it a few years later, because the pool of buyers for a studio is just not that large. Another story is that we worked with a client a while back who was hard-headed and did not want to take our advice. She ended up buying a house directly in front of a school on a busy road and in barely livable conditions. Unless she completely tears that house down and starts over, it will be very hard to sell down the road given its condition and location.

Mistake 3: Buying the Wrong House

The way you don't buy the wrong house is by looking at so many houses that you are almost sick of it. You should become an expert in the neighborhood. I would recommend spending a lot of time researching online as well as going to as many houses as possible – even the ones that you don't picture yourself buying – just so you can get an idea of what you like and dislike. You will often be surprised by different properties once you go out and see them in person; it happens all the time.

Mistake 4: Making Large Financial Changes While Under Contract

While you are under contract, you should make sure to keep your finances in the same shape as they were when you applied for the loan. That means, do not make any large purchases such as furniture, cars, and things of that nature. This can affect your ability to finance for the purchase price of your property. Also, be sure to not switch jobs – or even worse, lose your job – as that will cause your financing to get rejected and force you to back out of the contract. Celebrate after the purchase and buy all your furniture only after closing.

Mistake 5: Going With the Cheapest Option

When it comes to buying a house, you will have different options for agents, title companies, home inspectors, and more. There will often be a discount option for all of those services. I would recommend not going in that direction unless the person or company with the discount option has overwhelmingly positive reviews online and comes referred. There are often reasons why one service is significantly cheaper than another. I could tell you story after story about why you should not go with the cheapest lender, home inspector, or agent. Since this is such a large investment, you want to go with the best option – not the cheapest.

CHAPTER 4

House-Buying Myths

Buying Is Better Than Renting

Let me start this section by saying that more people have become millionaires through owning real estate than any other asset class. However, that is not to say that buying is always better than renting. If you are unsure of where you will live or only plan on staying somewhere for a couple years, then you should probably go with the flexibility of being a tenant instead of owning the property. Unless you plan to rent the house out for cash flow, buying only makes sense from a financial point of view if you plan on living in the house for several years – at least three, but better yet five or more. That is when you start to see appreciation and equity build up.

Real Estate Is a Good Long-Term Investment As It Always Goes Up

Throughout history, generally speaking, real estate does go up in value. However, it also depends on how long you hold on to your property. Over a long enough time horizon, nearly every property has gone up in value, but keep in mind that most people don't hold on to their properties forever – usually, it is more in the range of five, ten, fifteen, or sometimes 20+ years.

The real estate market is cyclical, so depending on where you buy in the market and when you are looking to sell it, the value of your property could have gone up or down. If resale value and long-term investment is at the top of your priority list, then you need to be sure that you are buying your house in a good location. I know that sounds obvious; however, I've seen it happen over and over again that a mediocre property in a great location will be worth significantly more than an amazing house in the middle of nowhere after a couple years. If you do plan on buying further outside of a city, just make sure there is some draw to the area, i.e. a major development or transportation hub.

The best place to buy if you are looking for an ROI is within 1 mile of a Whole Foods. You may have heard of the 'Whole Foods Effect', but basically they have done studies where properties within a short radius of a Whole Foods tend to appreciate significantly more than those outside of that radius. This could be for a number of factors; however, I would rely on the tens of millions of dollars that Whole Foods spends on research of the best neighborhoods and then piggyback off of their efforts. Whole Foods has a certain set of statistics and criteria that go into their location selections and are not always obvious to the average homebuyer.

A 30-Year Fixed Mortgage Is Always Best

30-year fixed mortgages are the most common type of loans that homebuyers get; however, that doesn't not necessarily mean they are the best. Believe it or not: there are many different types of loans with varying interest rates and payoff time frames that may suit you better.

One option is a 15-year mortgage, which obviously has higher monthly payments, but you will pay significantly less in interest and be done with the loan in half the time. Some people meet in the middle and get a 30-year loan with no prepayment penalty so that they have the option to pay it off in fifteen years or really any amount of time within the 30 years that they choose to.

Another option homebuyers have available are ARMs or adjustable rate mortgages for three, five, or seven years, where the interest rates for those years will be significantly lower than a traditional 30-year fixed. If you are planning on staying in the house for a shorter period of time, then this could be a great option for you. These types of loans are not utilized as much as they should be, and if you do your research on them, they could be a perfect fit for you.

Always Choose the Lender With the Lowest Rate

Choosing a mortgage and working with the right lender is similar to other things in business and life – just because it is the cheapest option with the lowest rate does not mean it is the best option for you. While I think you should shop around for the lowest rate, the highest likelihood of your offer being accepted usually comes from a local lender with a good reputation. The first thing many listing agents do when you submit an offer, is call your lender to make sure that you are qualified. The biggest turnoff for a listing agent is when they see a 1-800 number to an online lender halfway across the country and the phone is answered in a call center.

Although it might be the lowest rate, I have seen a lot of those deals fall apart because the lender is slower and not as concerned with getting the deal done as a local lender might be. I would recommend paying a little bit more and working with a lender nearby that you can talk to when needed and that comes highly recommended from other friends or agents. Especially if you are in a multiple-offer scenario, you want everything possible to be going in your favor, and having a good local lender can make a huge difference.

You Need a 20-Percent Down Payment

Many people think that when you buy a property, you always have to put down 20%. In expensive markets, that could be a fortune to most people. However, there are many different loan products where you can put down different amounts, as little as 3.5% if you are a first-time homebuyer and even 0% down if you are a veteran. If you put down less than 20%, you have to pay what's called PMI or private mortgage insurance, which usually adds a little bit to your monthly mortgage payment. However, in the big picture of your mortgage, it's a very small percent of the total. There are many loan options at 5% and 10% as well, so don't think that the 20% down is a requirement to buy a home.

Your Only Upfront Costs Are the Down Payment (Closing Costs)

When you start saving to buy a home, there will be down payment costs as well as closing costs, which are usually in the ballpark of 2.5 to 3.5%. The closing costs are an additional cost of pocket, i.e. not something that you can finance into your mortgage. Your closing costs pay for things like your mortgage application, survey, appraisal, property insurance, property taxes, title search, and other related title fees. Your title company and lender can provide you with an estimate early on in the process as to what your estimated fees are so that there are no surprises along the way.

The Asking Price Is Set in Stone

The asking price for real estate is definitely something that can be negotiable. In some instances it might make sense to even pay more than the asking price if it looks like a good deal, while in other cases you can even send in lowball offers. Agents typically do not like to work with people who lowball; however, if a property needs a lot of work or has been sitting on the market for a while, that could be a good opportunity to come in with a lower offer. Sometimes the seller is looking for terms and is not as concerned with price, so I've been in a situation where we could close sooner and were not asking for repairs, so we were able to buy the house at a much lower price than the other traditional offer that they had.

You Don't Need an Agent

Although being a real estate agent may seem like something anyone can do, I can assure you that it is much easier to buy a house with a good real estate agent than without one. Yes, anybody can let you in and show a house; however, the real reason you need an agent is so that you don't overpay, you submit offers in the correct way, you meet all your deadlines, and you have someone full time in the business advocating for you. Just make sure the agent comes recommended and has good reviews, and that you get along with them. I can't tell you how many times we've had unrepresented buyers trying to buy some of our listings. Within the first minute of talking to them, you can just tell that they are in way over their head and generally have no clue what they are doing.

School District Does Not Matter If You Have No Kids

In terms of resale value and the people that will be looking at buying your house down the road, the school district usually will play a factor. If you are just buying a one-bedroom condo, the district matters less, but if you are buying into a townhouse or single-family home, you should have a good understanding of how the school district is. Make sure the comps you are looking at are from the same school district and try to learn as much as possible about any future changes, good or bad, coming to the district. Sometimes, just one block away could be an amazing school district and vice versa. Do some research on school districts before buying so that you have a general understanding of the good and bad schools in your area. Keep in mind that school districts can change as well. If you live in an up-and-coming neighborhood with lots of development, chances are the school district will get better every year. It may be the worst district now, but five or ten years down the road it could be one of the best.

You Need to Get a Home Inspection

If you are a first-time homebuyer and you don't come from any type of construction or carpentry background, then I would almost always recommend a home inspection. If you are buying a single-family house or townhouse, an inspector usually has a list of items that need repair or updating, especially if it's an older home. In a lot of hot real estate markets across the country, it is becoming almost normal to waive the home inspection or just do a pass/fail inspection. If you are in a competitive market, I would recommend to do what's called a pre-inspection, where before you make your offer, you get an inspector into the house. Usually, inspections cost about $500; however, if the report comes back with just minor items, then when you make your offer, you can essentially waive your inspection and make your offer look much stronger in the eyes of the seller. You could also do what's called a pass/fail inspection where the inspector will do a normal inspection after getting the home under contract. Then it's up to you if you want to move forward or not after getting the report back. This offer also looks strong from the seller's standpoint since with a traditional home inspection a buyer will ask for numerous items to be fixed. I have seen pre-inspections, pass/fail inspections, as well as people having success waiving inspections completely. I would only recommend waiving the inspection if you are buying a condo, since there are significantly less potential issues, or if you come from a construction background and are comfortable making repairs.

You Can't Afford a Home

Many people think you need a small fortune saved up to be able to afford a house. However, there's a good chance that whatever you are paying in rent right now would be very similar to an actual mortgage payment. Not only that, but as a first-time homebuyer you can get many types of loans anywhere from 3.5 to 5% down, so you don't necessarily need to save up 20% like most people think. If you live in a city, Airbnb has become one of the most popular ways to afford a home. I know many people that have cut their mortgage in half or even more by renting out a room or two with Airbnb. This works best if you have some type of basement suite with a separate entrance that you can turn into a mini hotel. Either way, home ownership should not be thought of as something completely out of reach. I bought my first house on a 35K-a-year salary with 3.5% down (about 5K).

CHAPTER 5

Buying-a-House Checklist

We have covered a lot in this book. To recap the steps, in this chapter we will go over the buying-a-house checklist and reinforce everything you need to know. You should review this checklist several times and become an expert in the process.

1. Improve your finances as much as possible by saving money, paying down debt, and using a mortgage calculator to figure out how much you can afford.

2. Get a pre-approval with a local lender who comes referred and/or gets good reviews. Talk to at least 3 local lenders who have good reputations to find out what they offer.

3. Decide on what type of house you are looking for, whether that is a single-family house, townhouse, condo, etc., and what style of house you are looking for.

4. Look at different neighborhoods and decide where you want to live. Do as much research as you can on the neighborhoods online as well as by driving through them and walking around in them.

5. Find a good buyer's agent through referrals from friends and family, and then cross-reference the information with online reviews. You need someone who is responsive and whom you get along with.

6. Have your agent set you up with a listing search from the MLS that will send you any new properties, and browse through FSBOs. You should also be out there actively looking at open houses.

7. Once you have narrowed in on the type of house and neighborhood, have your agent send you any comps for the prospective property that will make an offer on. Review any disclosures and any other information the seller may have on renovations or updates.

8. Determine your price and what contingencies you would like to include, and make an offer. The common contingencies include a home inspection, appraisal, and financing. It is usually a negotiation, but sometimes if you make a good enough offer, then the seller will accept it straight up, and you can proceed to the next steps in the home-buying process.

9. If the seller accepts your offer, then you need to deposit your earnest money with the title

company, set up your inspection, and finalize your financing with your lender. The biggest things that happen after going under contract are the home inspection and working with your lender to make sure they have everything they need to close on time. Make sure to stay in constant communication with your lender, the title company, and your real estate agent.

10. Lastly, you will close the deal. You will receive the closing documents several days before closing to make sure that everything is correct. Make sure to bring a cashier's check and your ID to the closing. The title company will let you know the exact amount that you need to bring.

Conclusion

Overall, the home-buying process is a big deal. However, the more educated you are, the smoother the transaction will be. With buying a home, you want as many things as possible going for you, including being educated on the process, finding a good real estate agent, and using recommended vendors, such as home inspectors and title companies that have a good reputation. Buying a home can be a very rewarding experience, and after you complete the steps outlined in this book, you should go out and celebrate. You have made it to the finish line. Congratulations!

Resources and Next Steps

Are you looking to buy or sell a house in the Washington DC, Virginia, or Maryland area?

If so, please email me at info@actionhomebuyers.com with some basic information about what you are looking for and my team will be in touch to assist you. If you are looking to buy a house outside of the Washington DC metro area you can still email me and I will put you in touch with one of our recommended partners for your area of the country.

P.S. If you enjoyed this book I have a couple others on real estate investing that offer a ton of value and are available on Amazon in kindle, paperback, or audiobook version, whichever you prefer.

21 Ways to Find Off-Market Deals: This book gives you 21 proven strategies to finding lucrative off market deals that myself and other investors have used and continue to use to this day.

Probate Real Estate Investing: This book focuses on an overlooked and unique niche of real estate investing that has some of the best deals available in any market.

Off Market Real Estate Secrets: This book goes in depth on everything you need to know in the off market real estate world. It will open your eyes to deal-making possibilities.

For additional real estate tips you can subscribe to my YouTube channel at www.youtube.com/jeffleighton where I put out weekly videos on real estate investing.

I would also love to stay in touch via social media, connect with me below.

Instagram - http://www.instagram.com/j_late12
Snapchat - https://www.snapchat.com/add/jrl560
Facebook - https://www.facebook.com/jeff.leighton.5

Made in the USA
San Bernardino, CA
02 May 2018